THE
HORSE
IN
ACTION

THE
HORSE IN ACTION

Henry Wynmalen

In co-operation with

Michael Lyne

HAROLD STARKE LIMITED

By the same author

EQUITATION

RIDING FOR CHILDREN (Illustrated by Michael Lyne)

HORSE BREEDING AND STUD MANAGEMENT

DRESSAGE: A Study of the Finer Points of Riding

ISBN 0 287 69688 X

First published 1954
Reprinted 1956
Reprinted September 1964
Reprinted August 1973
© Henry Wynmalen 1954

Harold Starke Limited
14 John Street, London WC1N 2EJ
Printed and bound in England
by William Clowes & Sons, Limited
London, Beccles and Colchester

CONTENTS

INTRODUCTION *Page 9*

Chapter		*Page*
I	THE GAITS	14
II	THE WALK	16
The pure walk; the pace or amble; impure gaits; the near-amble, jogging; varying forms of the pure walk; the rein back.	
III	THE TROT	24
The pure gait; impure gaits; forging; ordinary, collected and extended trot; racing trot; racing "pace" or amble; the passage; the piaffe.	
IV	THE CANTER	36
Pure canter, in three time; impure canter, in four time; disunited canter.	

Chapter		*Page*
V	CHANGE OF LEG AT THE CANTER	42
The correct change; the disunited change; the change in front alone; the disunited canter.	
VI	THE GALLOP	47
quadrupedante putrem sonitu quatit ungula campum: Virgil. Pure gallop; disunited gallop.	
VII	THE JUMP	52
Sequence of hoofbeats; change of leg; interrupted rhythm.	
VIII	THE TRANSITIONS	58

ILLUSTRATIONS

THE PASSAGE *frontispiece*

	Page		Page
THE WALK—*seven figures*	15	TROTTERS AT RACING SPEED	31
THE PACE OR AMBLE—*six figures*	17	THE PIAFFE—*five figures*	33
VARYING FORMS OF WALK 1 Free Walk 2 Collected Walk 3 Walk of the High School Horse—*three figures*	19	PACERS AT RACING SPEED	34
		THE PASSAGE—*seven figures*	35
		THE CANTER—*eight figures*	37
FORMS OF IRREGULAR WALK AND JOGGING 1–3 Caused by nervous contraction 4–6 Relaxation is followed by return to real walk —*six figures*	21	IRREGULAR CANTER IN FOUR TIME Hind leg in advance; a fairly common fault denoting lack of impulsion at a slow canter —*eight figures*	39
THE REIN BACK—*nine figures*	23	IRREGULAR CANTER IN FOUR TIME Front leg in advance; a fault less commonly seen; note lateral support in fig. 4; the horse "rolls"	41
THE TROT—*seven figures*	25		
IRREGULAR TROT, FORELEG IN ADVANCE—*seven figures*	27	CORRECT CHANGE OF LEG—*ten figures*	43
IRREGULAR TROT, HIND LEG IN ADVANCE—*eight figures*	29	DISUNITED CHANGE OF LEG—*eight figures*	45
VARYING FORMS OF TROT 1 Ordinary 2 Collected 3 Extended —*three figures*	30	THE MOMENT OF SUSPENSION 1 not changing 2 changing correctly 3 changing disunited—*three figures*	46
		THE GALLOP—*twelve figures*	48

		Page
TRUE AND CONVENTIONAL FORM OF GALLOP—*six figures*		50
THE DISUNITED GALLOP—*seven figures*		51
STUDIES OF FREE-JUMPING HORSES —*seven figures*		54
HOOFBEATS DURING THE JUMP —*sixteen figures*		56
CHANGE OF LEG DURING THE JUMP —*twelve figures*		57
FROM HALT INTO WALK—*four figures*		59

		Page
FROM WALK INTO TROT—*five figures*		59
FROM TROT INTO WALK—*seven figures*		59
FROM TROT INTO CANTER—*six figures*		60
FROM CANTER INTO TROT—*six figures*		61
FROM WALK INTO CANTER—*five figures*		61
FROM CANTER INTO WALK—*five figures*		62
FROM HALT INTO CANTER—*six figures*		62
FROM CANTER INTO HALT—*seven figures*		63

INTRODUCTION

A SOUND KNOWLEDGE of the precise rhythm of a horse's action in all his paces is of paramount interest to the student of advanced horsemanship, to the instructor and to the equestrian artist.

It is a subject which has exercised the mind of man for fifty centuries at least. Indeed, it has come down to us that it was a matter of debate amongst the ancient Egyptians whether a trotting horse ever had all four legs off the ground during any moment of that gait; whether, in other words, there occurred a moment of suspension during the trot.

These and similar questions relating to the horse's gaits were to remain unanswered for thousands of years. Man had only his eye to rely on; and that, though able to convey an impressionist picture of movement, is quite incapable of arresting, and dissecting, the phases of it.

Now the trot is by far the simplest and the most regular of the horse's gaits. It becomes understandable then that the human eye, which failed to discover the moment of suspension of the trot, failed even more strikingly in analysing the much more complicated gaits of walk, canter, and gallop.

But the horse is a beautiful creature, and a romantic one, associated since time immemorial with all the glories of human pageantry. On account of his beauty, and of his association with man, the horse had to be depicted, through the ages, in every serviceable medium, in stone, in bronze and in paint. And most of these representations show the horse in his greatest and most striking point of beauty, in action!

In this way a tradition grew up of the moving horse, based originally on the eye's impression of movement and ultimately on what had become accepted as an artistically correct expression. With that we are all familiar, in historical statues, in paintings and in the numerous popular sporting prints.

It is now common knowledge that these traditional representations of the moving horse, notwithstanding their artistic merits and cultural interest, are factually misrepresentations of the moving horse. The horse just does not

9

move in that way. It is almost certain that quite a number of the great artists who fashioned their horses in the traditional manner must have had their doubts about the fidelity to nature of their presentations. The human mind, and the good artist's mind, is inquisitive and thirsts for knowledge as to what is and what is not true to nature. But though they may have had their doubts, they were without the means to solve such problems. Their eye was unable to arrest movement.

The fact that photography was used for this very purpose at a fairly early date proves that the need to put conventional ideas to the test had been felt; the distinction of first using photography for this purpose belongs to the American railway magnate Leland Stanford. Around the year 1872, he commissioned an American photographer, Eadweard Muybridge, to carry out the necessary experiments, and a doctor, J. B. D. Stillman, A.M., M.D., to analyse the results. It was nearly ten years before these experiments were completed and published in a most monumental book, *The Horse in Motion*, which appeared in Boston in 1882, and is now a rare volume.

Muybridge was obviously, in those early days, a photographer of exceptional ingenuity and skill, and who came very near to developing something that might have been a forerunner of the modern cinematographic camera. During the course of his experiments, begun with a single camera, he evolved a system, first of twelve cameras and subsequently of twenty-four, with which to take instantaneous photographs of moving horses.

His book contains a vast number of pictures obtained in this manner. They made a deep and lasting impression at the time. It could hardly have been otherwise, for they shattered the foundations of the conventional artistic representations for good and all.

Muybridge's conclusions were widely accepted and came to form the basis of current understanding of the horse's movements: they led also to the belief that the camera is a reliable and unfailing guide in the study of this subject.

But while Muybridge's photography was undoubtedly most ingenious, the conclusions drawn from it are incredibly inaccurate. The analysis made from a large number of pictures is totally erroneous: cantering horses are described indiscriminately as "fast walking" or "trotting"; similar mistakes abound; the authors are almost completely misled by their own instantaneous pictures.

More serious is that a considerable proportion of the

published figures depict animals which, forced into completely irregular deportment by obviously incompetent riders and drivers, go at distinctly impure gaits. Only in a few extreme cases do the authors themselves appear puzzled.

It is, of course, easy to understand that Muybridge and his collaborators, coming face to face for the first time in history with instantaneous pictures of arrested movements of a horse's action, were bound to make many misinterpretations. Even now, with three-quarters of a century's experience of horse photography, it is frequently extremely difficult to determine the precise action, or phase of action, depicted by certain photographs. To do so with accuracy demands a great deal of experience and special study.

Whilst the camera can determine momentary phases of a horse's action, it cannot correlate these phases, as the ciné-camera can. Even so, both the camera and the ciné-camera can only register what happens in front of their lenses, which may be correct action or may be faulty action. This is a most important distinction, which almost all photographers, following in Muybridge's footsteps, appear to have overlooked. The horse's action is a sequence of complicated motions in which, for one reason or another, many irregularities or impurities are liable to occur. It is largely due to failing to recognise this that so many misconceptions have found their way into present-day descriptions of the horse's gaits.

For—let there be no mistake about it—the general present day post-photographic knowledge of the horse's action is still far from accurate. To anyone intent on making a study of the subject, the many contradictions, inaccuracies and obvious mistakes to be found in current literature and art, can be most confusing and unsatisfactory.

It was not until I came into contact, some twenty years ago, with the analytical approach of the great Austrian painter of horses, Ludwig Koch (see *Die Reitkunst im Bilde*, Vienna, 1928), that I awoke to the necessity of studying innumerable pictures in order to learn to distinguish between regular, or pure, and accidental, irregular or impure, motions.

It is only by knowing the latter that the former can be reliably identified.

On account of these very irregularities, photography, whilst indispensable for study, is not a suitable medium for detailing the mechanism of the horse's gaits with unfailing clarity. In my opinion this can best be done graphically, by an artist's careful studies, and in this connection I consider myself fortunate in having awakened the interest of Michael Lyne and secured his help and close co-operation. It enables us to present to our readers an up-to-date and well-nigh exhaustive study of this very special subject, one that apparently has never been attempted in the English language.

Readers will appreciate that the intricacies of the subject are clarified much better by pictorial presentation than by the written word. Accordingly, the text of this book is meant to serve no other purpose than to clarify the message of the pictures where thought necessary.

In conclusion it should be stated that the regular gaits described are those shown by all sound and healthy horses of adequate conformation, moving in freedom under normal circumstances. Irregularity of gait occurs under saddle as the result of influences exerted by the rider, which prevent the horse from retaining his natural balance and with it the rhythm of his natural gaits. Irregularities occur, in other words, as a result of interference by the rider. Such interference may be momentary and accidental and cause a purely incidental disturbance of the gait for one or two strides, which is, of course, of little moment.

But horses, ridden habitually under the effect of such disturbing interference will attempt to minimize the discomfort felt by taking avoiding action, which they can only do by altering their natural attitude and carriage at the expense of balance and rhythm. This may quite easily lead to impurity of gait, and if the horse be ridden long enough under similar conditions the impurity may become habitual.

Though forms of interference by the rider occur even at a walk, they are more often seen, and the results more noticeable, at the faster gaits of trot and canter. At these, moving in freedom, the horse carries his head so that its highest point is at the poll, with the crest of the neck rounded and with the nose at a natural angle somewhat in front of the vertical, the mouth approximately level with the withers and the head kept still. This correct and natural form of headcarriage is an obvious characteristic of the balanced horse, whether in freedom or under saddle.

There are a variety of reasons that may cause difficulty in maintaining correct balance under saddle. Within the compass of this book the principal reason only can be referred to, that being the use made of the bridle. Its correct use is the greatest difficulty in riding. It cannot be mastered without good hands. Hands transmit messages from the rider's to the horse's brain via the animal's mouth and, unless the rider has a sympathetic understanding of the sensitiveness of that mouth, he will hurt it. The message will be blurred and the horse will take avoiding action in order to reduce the pain inflicted. He does that by altering the position of his head, in the attempt to escape or to reduce the pressure of the bridle on his bars. More often than not, he will lift his head and mouth above the bridle, resulting, in extreme cases, in a ewe-neck. The lifting of the head affects the normal distribution of weight, and with it the balance; it also causes the back to dip, impeding the action of the loins and with it, of course, that of the hind legs.

It is only too easy to provoke in this and similar ways impurity of gait by inappropriate use of the bridle, and the impurity may in course of time become so pronounced as to become almost akin to lameness. Horses so affected are then said to be bridle-lame.

Chapter I

THE GAITS

THIS BOOK is concerned with a description of the horse's regular gaits. These are, in the first place, the walk, the trot, the canter and the gallop. But attention must be given also to the pace, or amble; though seldom seen in England the amble is the fundamental gait of certain breeds and types of horses; it occurs also, occasionally, as an irregular and therefore faulty gait in certain animals who are not, by breeding or special training, true amblers.

In considering the true gaits of the horse we are concerned mainly with the pure form of each of them; but it is important to be able to detect impurities when they occur and an attempt is therefore made to represent also the more likely forms which these aberrations may take and to point to some of the reasons which may lead to them. To know the cause is often half the remedy.

It is the accepted custom to define a horse's gaits by mentioning the "leading foreleg". It is a custom so long established, and in such general use, that it would assuredly be a hopeless task to try to alter the horseman's language in this respect. Besides, it does not seem to matter very much, as long as it can be understood that this established terminology is actually a misnomer.

The use of terms to describe a horse's gait goes back centuries, and descriptions are based upon that which it is easiest for the human eye to discern, and that is, without a doubt, the horse's front leg. It is natural enough, therefore, to detail, as is customary, the mechanism of any particular gait with the movement of a front leg.

But, though natural, it is by no means logical! For a horse standing still in a normally balanced position begins his every movement with a hind leg; it is from there that all propulsion emanates; the forelegs merely follow suit.

Whilst I do not therefore propose to deviate in any way from the customary terms, such as "canter with the near fore leading", I do intend to be logical and to identify in each case the particular hind leg from which any given movement originates.

THE WALK

Chapter II

THE WALK

*THE PURE WALK; THE PACE OR AMBLE; IMPURE GAITS; THE NEAR-AMBLE,
JOGGING; VARYING FORMS OF THE PURE WALK; THE REIN BACK*

THE WALK is a "pace of four-time". Four distinct hoofbeats are heard to every stride as each foot in turn strikes the ground; each foot strikes the ground by itself and never in combination or together with any other foot.

The sequence of the hoofbeats is: (1) near hind, (2) near fore, (3) off hind, (4) off fore.

The sequence at the pure walk is therefore "lateral", in that both feet to one side of the horse meet the ground before both feet to the other side follow suit; but the sequence is "lateral-consecutive" since no two such feet ever do so simultaneously.

Picture 1 on page 15 shows the commencement of the stride; the near hind delivers the impulsion, the near fore stretches forward to follow suit, whilst the off hind is in motion to be brought forward in its turn.

It is valuable to study from the pictures, in addition to the sequence of the hoofbeats, the sequence of the supports. Thus in picture 1, the commencement of the stride from a halt, we have diagonal support on two legs, near hind and off fore; followed by triangular support, as soon as the near fore touches the ground, on near hind and both front legs; followed by lateral support on two legs, near hind and near fore; followed by triangular support, on near fore and both hind legs this time; followed by diagonal support once more, this time off hind and near fore, and so on in regular sequence.

That regular sequence is the essence of the pure gait. Whenever the regular sequence, "earmarked" by the four hoofbeats at precisely equal intervals and regular tempo, is lost, any pretence at a pure gait is lost with it; the horse is no longer "walking".

The pace or amble is a gait closely allied to the walk, since both gaits are lateral. But, as has been seen, the

THE PACE OR AMBLE

hoofbeats at the walk are "lateral consecutive", and, in contrast, the hoofbeats of the pace or amble are "lateral simultaneous", since each lateral pair of feet, near hind and near fore followed by off hind and off fore, always touch down together. Two hoofbeats are heard to each stride; the amble is a "pace of two-time".

In the walk, support is alternatively on two feet and on three feet; the support on two feet alternates between diagonal and lateral.

In the amble the support is always on two feet and is always lateral.

It is to be noted that a horse moving at walking speed, whether at the pure walk or at the amble, has never less than two feet in contact with the ground; there never occurs a moment when only one leg is in support, nor a moment of suspension when all legs are in the air.

But, as has been seen, walk and amble, being both lateral gaits, are closely akin. The lateral gait is not "unnatural" to the horse. This explains why it has been found comparatively simple to "teach" horses to amble, a very common practice in the Middle Ages and indeed much later than that. The amble was, especially in Spain, considered the favourite gait for a lady's mount. The reason is not far to seek. The confirmed ambler retains the same gait at trotting speed, at which he can move very fast indeed. This fast amble feels from the saddle much like a slight rocking movement, with some swing to it, and is, especially for a lady riding side-saddle, far more comfortable and less strenuous than a fast trot; long distances can be covered at considerable speed with little fatigue.

Apart from training horses to amble, horses were bred to amble, and to this date certain breeds and families of horses remain to whom the amble is the natural pace. The pacing horses of Peru and Mexico, descended from Spanish-Oriental ancestry, and the racing pacers of France and of the U.S.A. are well-known examples; in England too some racing pacers still remain.

It cannot have been unduly difficult to produce amblers by selective breeding, since amblers may occasionally occur in horses which by descent should be pure walkers.

This leads to consideration of various forms of impure, irregular or faulty walking. Some horses, whose natural gait is the pure walk, may assume the amble or a near-amble. The real amble, a pure lateral pace of two-time, is easy enough to distinguish. But in the near-amble the

VARYING FORMS OF WALK

1 Free Walk 2 Collected Walk 3 Walk of the High School Horse

horse still goes in a pace of four-time, but loses the regular tempo; the hoofbeats no longer occur at precisely regular intervals; those of each lateral pair of legs come very close together and there is an interval before the hoofbeats of the opposing lateral pair, also very close together, occur.

It is a distinctly faulty gait; the horse is hurrying. The cure, which may be difficult, is to eliminate the cause of the hurry.

Jogging, instead of walking, is a frequent fault. Usually one imagines that the horse is executing a trotting movement at walking, or rather less than walking, speed. But jogging is not as a rule a true trot, diagonal, in pace of two-time. It is often done at an amble, a near-amble or some other wholly irregular form of impure trot.

In a sense every pure gait, but in particular the walk, demands a degree of relaxation on the part of the horse. If such relaxation is lost, tenseness will occur, causing the horse to lose the tempo and normal purity of his gait.

Weakness or tiredness may be the cause, but over-excitement is the more frequent reason. Such excitement is often enhanced and may even be wholly caused by faulty riding and training; the horse that cannot go freely forward into his bridle will avoid doing so either by over-bending behind the bridle or else by avoiding the pressure on the bars by star-gazing; such horses are apt to go tense and to jog on the slightest provocation.

The cure is encouragement of relaxation, allowing the horse to lengthen himself, to stretch head and neck, and inducing him, by sparse and careful use of a light and comfortable snaffle, to confident acceptance (Page 19).

Sometimes a collected horse is seen being schooled to some such movement as a walk on two tracks, or a half pass, assuming the two-time diagonal pace of the pure trot; such movement, though in itself a perfectly pure pace, is then faulty because it is not a walk.

The pure walk may be seen in a number of forms, varying from the long stride of the freely extended horse, through the rather more collected form of the made hunter or hack, to the completely collected form of the very highly schooled horse. But the difference is only in the outward shape of the horse; he assumes a more upright position, his hind legs tread further under the body, the steps become shorter and a little more elevated, all this occurring gradually as the collection increases.

But whatever the degree of collection may be, the

1

2

3

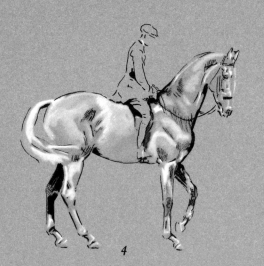

4

5

6

FORMS OF IRREGULAR WALK AND JOGGING
1–3 Caused by nervous contraction
4–6 Relaxation is followed by return to real walk

strictly even tempo in four-time, "lateral consecutive", must be maintained since without this the horse is no longer "walking".

The rein back is an unnatural movement to the horse. He will very seldom use it of his own volition, and then only when there is no other way open to him to extricate himself from some tight corner.

He cannot step back at the four-time pace of the walk; he can only do so at the two-time diagonal pace of the trot, near hind and off fore together and off hind and near fore in unison. The movement is always somewhat awkward to him; good horsemanship requires it to be done slowly and deliberately and never more than a few steps at the time; six steps should be the maximum.

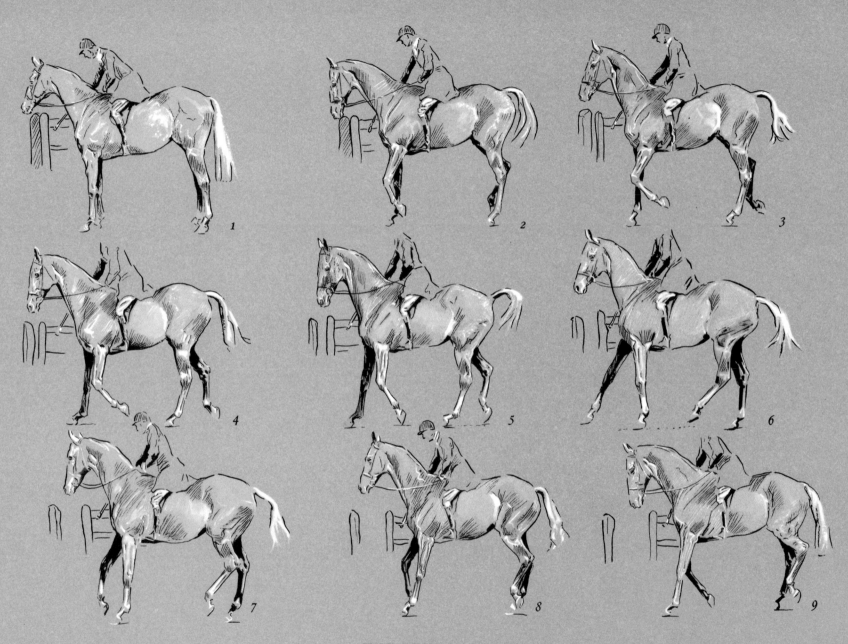

THE REIN BACK

Chapter III

THE TROT

THE TROT is a "pace of two-time"; we hear two hoofbeats to every stride as each diagonal pair of legs, near hind and off fore followed by off hind and near fore, strike the ground.

It has been seen that a horse at the walk never has, during any time of the movement, less than two legs in contact with the ground. At the trot this is no longer so.

At the trot, with say the left diagonal (near fore and off hind) in support, the horse swings forward and advances the right diagonal (off fore and near hind) before taking off, or in a sense jumping off the ground, when there follows a moment of suspension before this right diagonal in its turn touches the ground. During this moment of suspension all four legs are off the ground, or in the air.

The trot can only be considered pure as long as each diagonal pair of legs moves simultaneously with absolute precision so that only one hoofbeat is heard as each pair strikes the ground, and thus only two hoofbeats per completed stride. The trot is "diagonal simultaneous".

If more than two distinct hoofbeats are heard one or the other of the following types of impure gait is being witnessed:

(1) the forelegs are in advance of the diagonally corresponding hind legs, or

(2) the hind legs are in advance of the diagonally corresponding forelegs, or

(3) the hind legs are doing a canter stride with the forelegs trotting.

In the former two cases a double beat is heard, very close together yet sufficiently distinct, as each diagonal pair of legs meets the ground in close succession but not absolutely simultaneously.

In the third case three beats are heard, and accordingly

THE TROT

this faulty gait is known in some languages as "three-beat" (Dutch: *drieslag*, German: *dreischlag*).

The first impure gait, front leg in advance of the corresponding hind leg, and the third, the "three-beat", often merge into one another. It may be seen in fast trotting horses which are driven, or ridden, beyond their balance, when the hind legs fail to keep up the tempo. It is seen in racing trotters and also seen in the extended trot of certain ridden horses pushed beyond their true capacity; in the latter case this is, of course, a very serious fault.

The other impure gait, hind leg in advance of the corresponding front leg, is met in the case of star-gazers either ridden or driven, in the latter case frequently due to an overtight bearing rein. Such horses go, or are forced to go, with a rigid back and stiff loins which cannot swing; hence the impurity of gait. Stiffness through age and wear may cause the same trouble.

In figures 3 and 8 on page 29, the precise moment of the trot can be seen at which near hind and near fore, or, as the case may be, off hind and off fore, come closest together. As long as the gait is pure this near fore (with its diagonal companion off hind) leaves the ground before that near hind touches down. But if that near hind is sufficiently in advance of the correct tempo, or the near fore behind its tempo which amounts to the same thing, these two feet may clash and "forge", as the peculiar noise is called which results from the knock of a shoe of the hind foot against that of the front foot.

This forging can happen when the horse is driven faster at the trot than his abilities allow, causing him to lose the proper tempo of his gait, the while announcing his distress for all the world to hear.

But as a rule there is evidence of this at quite an ordinary pace; it is then a sign of lack of balance, lack of swing, of energy and impulsion, usually due to weakness and poor conditions.

The amble has already been described as a pace of two-time wherein the legs are moved in lateral pairs. It has then been observed that in the amble at walking speed the horse always has two legs in contact with the ground. In the amble at trotting speed, that is no longer so; as in the trot, there is a distinct moment of suspension, with all four legs in the air, as the horse takes off from the ground with one lateral pair of legs and before the other pair touches down.

It will be appreciated that the trot and the amble, being

IRREGULAR TROT, FORELEG IN ADVANCE

paces of two-time wherein the horse always moves his legs in pairs, diagonal in the one case and lateral in the other, are the easiest paces to define and also to recognise from a picture or a photograph; in particular if it is remembered that, since the legs are moved in pairs, such legs are always parallel to each other. This parallel position of any given pair of legs occurs in no other pace. If this is borne in mind confusion need never be caused by photographs or pictures of horses at a highly collected walk, with much elevation, which can look very "trot-like" if showing the horse with a diagonal in support. If the horse is taken at the walk, neither the supporting diagonal nor the other pair of legs will be parallel.

As with the walk, the pure trot is to be seen in a number of different forms, which must all, to be considered pure, satisfy the essential requirements of being diagonal, in perfect two-time, and with a moment of suspension.

In everyday riding the ordinary trot, the collected trot and the extended trot may be seen. In the ordinary trot the horse moves easily and quietly in his natural cadence with a comfortable head-carriage, well in front of the vertical. In the collected trot the hind legs tread somewhat farther under the body, the head is carried a shade higher and nearer the vertical and the gait, though somewhat slower and with shorter strides, is a shade more brilliant and accentuated. In the extended trot the horse lengthens himself, stretches head and neck forward and lengthens his stride appreciably (Pages 30 and 31).

The racing trot shows the maximum extension and speed of which horses bred and trained for this particular purpose are capable. The energy of this racing gait is tremendous, as may be judged from the distance travelled "in the air" during the moment of suspension, and by the considerable height at which the suspension can be seen. It is also true of the racing "pace" or amble.

In high school riding two further forms of the trot are met, the passage and the piaffe (Pages 35 and 33).

The passage is an exceedingly highly collected trot, wherein the horse moves with tremendous energy, in a slow and very deliberate cadence, raising each diagonal in turn high off the ground, remaining distinctly suspended in the air for a moment, at appreciable height, between every two hoofbeats. The action in front and behind should be of equal brilliance and energy, the hind legs treading well under the body, head and neck carried high, very well bridled, and very light in hand. The impression

IRREGULAR TROT, HIND LEG IN ADVANCE

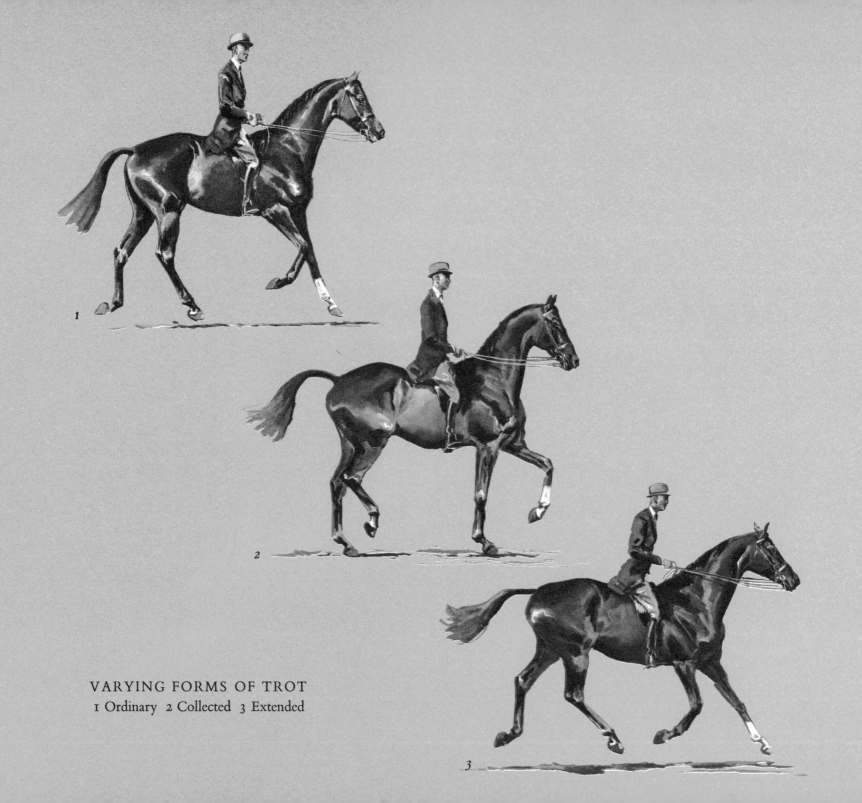

VARYING FORMS OF TROT
1 Ordinary 2 Collected 3 Extended

TROTTERS AT RACING SPEED

made should be one of almost effortless grace, the horse brilliant but completely calm. The horse moves forward slowly, dancing as it were from one diagonal on to the other.

The piaffe is a passage done on the same spot, the horse trotting in the cadence of the passage without advancing. It constitutes the most difficult form of trot of which a horse can be made capable, and requires the absolute maximum combination of collection and impulsion that it is possible to achieve.

The horse cannot be brought to the correct performance of these airs unless and until he has achieved, through years of careful and methodical training, the superlative balance and command of his limbs that results from complete suppleness of every muscle.

It is important to observe that these two airs, which constitute the highest form of perfection to which the horse can be brought at any of his natural gaits, are achieved at the trot. It is the horse's most rhythmic gait, and the one at which he achieves perfect balance and carriage more easily than at any other. As such, the achievements of a good trot is the very basis of all good riding.

1   2   3

4   5

THE PIAFFE

PACERS AT RACING SPEED

1

2

3

4

7

6

5

THE PASSAGE

Chapter IV

THE CANTER

PURE CANTER, IN THREE-TIME; IMPURE CANTER, IN FOUR-TIME;
DISUNITED CANTER

IN MANY LANGUAGES there is no such distinctive term as that by which, in England, the canter and the gallop is distinguished. Admittedly the two modes of propulsion are so clearly allied that they merge into one another as the pace increases or decreases.

Basically they do not constitute two different gaits; but they are most certainly two different varieties of gait, since the sequence of the footfalls is not the same.

The canter, or slow gallop, is a pace of three-time, in which three hoofbeats occur to each stride. There is a distinction between canter with the "near fore" and canter with the "off fore" leading.

In the canter with the "off fore" leading, the sequence is: (1) near hind, (2) diagonal comprising off hind and near fore together, (3) off fore, followed by suspension "in the air" and coming down on off hind again.

In the canter with the "near fore" leading the sequence is,

of course, reversed and becomes: (1) off hind, (2) near hind and off fore, (3) near fore followed by suspension.

We notice that the leg seen as the leading front leg is actually the last leg to come down, after the moment of suspension, before the new stride commences with the off hind touching down.

We notice further that the canter is, like the trot, a diagonal movement. But, whereas the trot is a symmetric diagonal movement, in which both diagonal pairs of legs act in precisely the same manner, the canter is an asymmetric diagonal movement in which the so-called leading foreleg and its companion diagonal hind leg act independently, since their respective hoofbeats are separated by the combined hoofbeat of the other diagonal, which acts in unison.

Thus the single hoofbeat of the non-leading diagonal is preceded by the hoofbeat of the opposing hind leg and

THE CANTER

followed by that of the opposing front leg, which is called the leading leg. As in the trot the two legs that act in unison, the non-leading pair, are therefore always parallel, whereas the leading pair are not.

Once we can see the picture in this way we will find it easier to distinguish and to recollect the correct sequence.

It is peculiar to the canter that the horse can use either of the diagonal pair of legs in the manner described, resulting accordingly in either the canter with the off fore leading or in the canter with the near fore leading.

In the canter with the near fore leading the sequence is, of course, reversed and becomes: (1) off hind, (2) near hind and off fore, (3) near fore followed by suspension.

The essence of a pure canter is the cadence in three-time.

The moment this three-time cadence is lost the pace becomes impure; a canter in four-time, which is sometimes seen, is faulty.

It may occur in the very slow, collected or school canter. The slower the pace, the greater the impulsion required to maintain purity of gait.

Referring to the picture of the pure canter, it will be seen that the horse, when taking off with the near hind leg, must use considerable energy in lifting the whole length of his body, from loins to forehand, to some considerable height, while propelling himself forward at the same time some considerable distance so that the off hind and near fore shall touch down simultaneously. Incidentally this implies the need to maintain, even at the very slowest paces, a relatively great length of stride: the tempo becomes slower rather than the stride shorter.

If the horse fails to deliver the degree of impulsion needed to maintain correct length of stride and tempo, either through lack of energy on his part or on that of his rider, the sequence of hoof beats will become: (1) near hind, (2) off hind, (3) near fore, (4) off fore, suspension. So, instead of a three-time gait, we now have a four-time gait. This faulty gait is illustrated on page 39, and it will be seen that the unity of action of the non-leading diagonal off hind and near fore is disturbed both ways: the off hind touches down and also takes off "in advance" of its companion front leg; the perfect parallel position, which this diagonal should maintain, is likewise disturbed.

Badly-balanced horses, those that go on the forehand, those who trail their quarters behind instead of bringing them well under the body, are liable to show a different kind of defective canter in four-time, in which the front

IRREGULAR CANTER IN FOUR TIME
Hind leg in advance; a fairly common fault denoting lack of impulsion at a slow canter

leg of the non-leading diagonal touches down and takes off "in advance" of its companion hind leg. The sequence then becomes (1) near hind, (2) near fore, (3) off hind, (4) off fore, suspension.

The most faulty gait of all is the disunited canter. In the canter it occurs seldom, except as the result of a badly executed change of leg. At the gallop the disunited gait occurs more frequently. For the sake of clarity and brevity therefore, our more detailed discussion will be taken in conjunction with these movements.

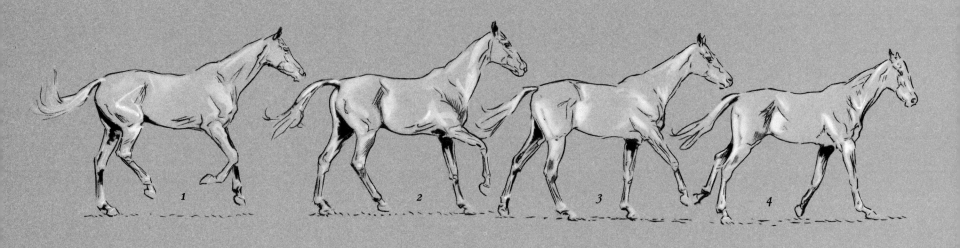

IRREGULAR CANTER IN FOUR TIME
Front leg in advance; a fault less commonly seen; note lateral support in Fig. 4: the horse "rolls"

Chapter V
CHANGE OF LEG AT THE CANTER

THE CORRECT CHANGE; THE DISUNITED CHANGE; THE CHANGE IN FRONT ALONE;
THE DISUNITED CANTER

THE PERFECTLY executed change of leg at the canter is done by the horse during the moment of suspension; accordingly the change is known as "change in the air".

The perfect change is depicted on page 43. Figures 1, 2, 3 and 4 show the horse cantering with the off fore leading; in figure 4 the horse is just taking off for the moment of suspension, shown in figure 5; it is during this one brief moment of suspension that the change takes place; in figure 6 we see the horse touch down on the off hind (as compared with the near hind in figure 1), with the near fore coming into the lead (as against the off fore in figure 1).

The change is therefore complete; the horse has changed behind (!) and in front simultaneously.

This correct change is perfectly fluent, balanced and easy; the tempo and cadence of the gait is not interrupted or disturbed in any way; the horse neither accelerates nor decelerates; the movement is only barely discernible to the rider, whose comfortable position in the saddle is not affected.

Unfortunately the change so done demands complete unity between horse and rider and constitutes a feat of refined horsemanship. It is not easy to effect one correct change, and to effect a number of changes at close or very close intervals is very difficult indeed.

The change in the air is a subtle movement of great delicacy and the least interference by the rider with the horse's balance or unhindered progress may result in a faulty change.

The fault most commonly seen is that whereby the horse, instead of changing behind (!) and in front simultaneously, changes first in front and then behind. During the moment of suspension, in which he is supposed to

CORRECT CHANGE OF LEG

change all round, he changes in front only; the proper sequence, cadence and progress of the canter are all interrupted, since the horse is for the moment, disunited; the change of the hind legs will follow either while the horse has both front legs in support or else during the next phase of suspension; either way the change is "disunited".

Either way there is a great loss of balance and interruption of progress; the horse half stops, the rider receives a considerable jolt, perhaps forcing him to stand in the stirrups, the change is rough and, frankly, a failure.

The manner this faulty change occurs is shown on page 45. Again figures 1, 2, 3 and 4 show the horse cantering correctly with the off fore leading and figure 5 shows the horse in the air. Figure 6 shows the near fore coming into the lead, the horse having changed in front, but touching down again, as in figure 1 on the near hind; the horse not having changed behind; figure 7 shows the horse disunited and the disturbance of his progress.

It is thus obvious that the fault, if fault there is to be,

occurs during the moment of suspension; for further clarification three pictures on page 46 show the moment of suspension; all relate to the same horse cantering with the off fore leading during the stride preceding the moment of suspension. Figure 1 shows the horse in the air "not changing"; figure 2 shows the horse changing correctly behind (!) and in front simultaneously; figure 3 shows the faulty change, in front only and not behind.

A more serious fault than the disunited change, and one to be seen all too frequently in our show rings, is the change in front alone; the change behind does not take place at all so that, after the change in front, the horse keeps on cantering disunited.

In the disunited canter the diagonal action of the true canter, and with it the simultaneous support on one diagonal, are lost. Consequently there can be no longer any question of a three-time movement; the disunited canter proceeds in four-time; it is an irregular, exceedingly undesirable gait.

DISUNITED CHANGE OF LEG

THE MOMENT OF SUSPENSION
1 not changing; *2* changing correctly;
3 changing disunited

Chapter VI

THE GALLOP

Quadrupedante putrem sonitu quatit ungula campum: Virgil

PURE GALLOP; DISUNITED GALLOP

I T HAS already been seen that the gallop and the canter are closely allied gaits. In fact they are basically the same gait, since characterized by the identical type of diagonal action. In the gallop there is, as in the canter, the leading diagonal, say near hind and off fore, and the non-leading diagonal, say off hind and near fore. And, as in the canter, the hoofbeats of the non-leading diagonal are preceded by that of the opposite hind leg and followed by that of the leading foreleg.

But whereas the canter is a pace of three-time, the gallop is a pace of four-time; in the canter the non-leading diagonal makes one simultaneous hoofbeat, whereas in the gallop the same diagonal makes two consecutive hoofbeats. In the canter three legs are in support twice, at the second and at the third tempo of the pace; in the gallop there are never more than two legs in support.

The canter is a comparatively collected pace, in which the horse's position is a fairly upright one, with the fore-hand carried high and with the head carried high on a curved neck. The gallop is a fully extended pace, the horse stretched level to his full length, forehand carried level with the ground, with the head stretched forward. The strides reach their maximum length and the three-time tempo of the canter is no longer adequate. So the gallop becomes a pace of four-time; once more taking for our example a horse galloping with the off fore leading, the following is the sequence: (1) near hind, (2) off hind, (3) near fore, (4) off fore, suspension. Virgil's quotation at the head of this chapter proves that the Romans were well aware of the "four-time" character of the gallop. The gait is illus-trated·on page 48.

It is interesting to compare those illustrations which depict the gallop as the pace really is with the conventional presentation of the old sporting print; in so doing we may

THE GALLOP

as well reflect that this conventional presentation is not by any means completely a thing of the past; we may still see fairly modern, and occasionally even contemporary, illustrations which are very little different (Page 50).

The following are the crucial points to note.

The conventional picture will show the horse at full stretch whilst in the air. Actually the horse, whilst in the air, is not stretched at all but has on the contrary all four legs right underneath himself.

The conventional picture will show two front legs fully stretched forward at the same time. Actually this never occurs, and whenever both front legs are showing towards the front more or less together, at least one hind leg is on the ground at the same time.

The conventional picture will also show two hind legs fully stretched backwards at the same time. Actually this position does occur, but only while at least one front leg is on the ground at the same time.

Mention has been made already of the disunited canter, which is comparatively rare.

The disunited gallop is comparatively more common. It is frequently due to the attempt of a tired horse to change the leading foreleg; whilst such horses can and will occasionally change all round, that is behind and in front, it is more usual to see them change disunited, in front only, and to see them continue galloping disunited (Page 51).

The sequence of the disunited gallop, the horse leading with the off fore, is: (1) off hind, (2) near hind, (3) near fore, (4) off fore. As observed already in the previous chapter, the diagonal character of the true gallop is lost, the disunited gallop is a lateral pace.

It is an irregular gait, causing loss of tempo and of true balance; resulting in reduced safety and increased strain on the animal's limbs. When a horse is said to have lost a race "because he changed leg", it usually means that he disunited himself.

TRUE AND CONVENTIONAL FORM OF GALLOP

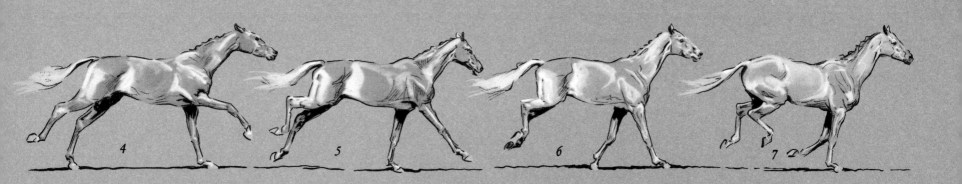

THE DISUNITED GALLOP

Chapter VII

THE JUMP

SEQUENCE OF HOOFBEATS; CHANGE OF LEG; INTERRUPTED RHYTHM

THE HORSE can only give of his best as long as his balance and the rhythm of his progress are not disturbed. This applies to the horse's every movement, not even excluding the walk, but it applies in particular to the jump.

It is difficult enough for the rider to avoid causing some such disturbance occasionally on the level, even at the walk; it is quite impossible for anyone, however expert, never to be caught out during a jump. There are in fact but few riders who do not hinder the horse in some degree, however slight, in the maximum amount of freedom which the horse requires in order to jump with the maximum of ease.

These optimum conditions are fulfilled for certain only when the horse jumps loose and in full freedom. It is only by studying the horse's jumping under those conditions that one arrives at a true picture of the ideal form of jumping. Once the horseman understands this form he will be prepared to try and emulate it as nearly as a good horseman can.

Observe, then, from the pictures of our free-jumping horses how the horse drops his quarters, the tremendous effort of his loins, the manner in which he bends his back; let us appreciate that it is the loins and the back that supply the major effort; but above all observe how tremendously the horse stretches himself in length, reaching forward and downwards as far as possible with head and neck.

It is not difficult to see that the rider who wishes to equal or even to approach this ideal form must avoid, as best he can, hindering the muscular play of loins and back and that he must try, in particular, to ensure freedom of head and neck.

The pictures show clearly that the jump is in essence no other than a gallop stride; it follows that the gallop, or the canter, is the horse's natural gait when approaching a jump; it is the gait he will choose unfailingly if the choice be left to him. As far as he is concerned there is no material difference between canter and gallop; there is only a matter of changing the timing of his hoofbeats, which he can do without effort and without change of balance. This is no longer so at the trot, and the change from trot into gallop at the very moment of the take-off does impose an extra effort on the horse. In a general way it is better to avoid jumping from a trot, though the latter exercise may have its uses, over small fences, if it is desired to control too much impetuosity in the approach.

In the illustrations, then, the horse approaches the jump in the gallop with the off fore leading; so it is known that the sequence of hoofbeats will be (1) near hind, (2) off hind, (3) near fore, (4) off fore, suspension. The last stride of the approach is the take-off stride, when the following occurs: as the non-leading near fore meets the ground (tempo 3), the horse applies a momentary brake to his progress, raises head and shoulders, all in order to bring his hind legs much farther under his body; or in other words he collects himself; next the leading foreleg (tempo 4) meets the ground, exactly as in an ordinary gallop stride, and the horse lifts himself into the suspension, to go over the jump this time, off the leading foreleg, again exactly as in an ordinary gallop stride; next the near hind (tempo 1), followed immediately by the off hind (tempo 2) come into contact with the ground, delivering the impulsion for the jump.

Next, on the landing side of the obstacle, it is the near fore (tempo 3), which is the first to touch down, followed immediately by the off fore (tempo 4). And, once more exactly as in the gallop stride pure and simple, the horse begins the period of suspension from this off fore and is "in the air" once more before the hind legs touch down in the normal sequence, near hind, (tempo 1) and off hind (tempo 2).

It is well known that horses may change legs during the jump. This occurs in the same manner exactly as already described in Chapter V. Thus the horse which leads with the off fore will begin the period of suspension from that particular leg (tempo 4); having changed during the jump however, he will now land on the same leg (tempo 3!), and the near fore has now become the leading leg (tempo 4); provided the change is perfect the hind legs have changed as well, so that the off hind becomes tempo 1 and the near hind tempo 2.

But although the jump does not affect the sequence of the horse's hoofbeats from those of the uninterrupted gallop, it does considerably affect the rhythm of the pace,

STUDIES OF
FREE-JUMPING HORSES

or rather its smooth continuity. We have already seen that the horse brakes powerfully during the take-off stride; that he shortens himself and drops his quarters low in order to engage his hind legs fully. He then accelerates with powerful impulse over the obstacle, lengthening himself to his full extent. On landing there is again a moment of retardation and collection, which permits him once more to engage his hind legs very fully in order to deliver the extra effort needed for the next following gallop stride.

The take-off, the landing and the resumption of the pace from the landing stride all impose a great effort on the horse, in which all elements of his body play their important part. Any interference by the rider liable to hinder the horses's liberty of action or his balance is seriously detrimental.

HOOFBEATS DURING THE JUMP

CHANGE OF LEG DURING THE JUMP

Chapter VIII

THE TRANSITIONS

THE HORSE in freedom performs the transitions from one gait into another in a smooth and effortless manner. In the case of the ridden horse such smoothness becomes a mark of the rider's ability and of the stage of the horse's training.

The horse at liberty will usually move from the halt into a walk, from the walk into a trot, from the trot into a canter, and vice versa; but he can change even direct from walk into canter just as easily. The transitions from the halt into a canter or gallop may be effected so rapidly that the preparatory walk or trot stride is hardly discernible; but it is there just the same, for to jump off from standing still, into a canter or a gallop, is not natural to the horse.

With the ridden horse then, it is sound horsemanship to follow the precepts of nature and to take the horse from a halt into a gallop, and reversely from a gallop into a halt, by going progressively and smoothly through the intermediate paces. A rider should be able to do so on any horse that has been reasonably well schooled for ordinary outdoor riding purposes.

To be able to take the horse neatly from a walk into a canter and from a canter into a walk without intermediate trot steps already demands a much higher degree of schooling and ability.

To canter on from the halt, or from the rein back, belongs to advanced riding and to achieve a nice, easy and smooth halt direct from the canter is a delicate feat of horsemanship that can be expected only from the fully schooled horseman on the fully schooled horse.

The illustrations show just how these various transitions occur.

FROM HALT INTO WALK

WALK INTO TROT

TROT INTO WALK

FROM TROT INTO CANTER

FROM CANTER INTO TROT

FROM WALK INTO CANTER

FROM CANTER INTO WALK

FROM HALT INTO CANTER

FROM CANTER INTO HALT